Y0-DJP-778

A LOOK AROUND THE SOVIET UNION

y Dr. Margaret Holland

PHOTO CREDITS: **Soviet Life Magazine:** front cover (ice skaters) and back cover, pages 3, 4, 5, 9 (three girls), (old man), 18 (sheep), 20, 21, 26, 27, 30, 31. **Sovfoto/Eastfoto:** pages 10, 11 (Red Square and Palace of Congresses), 4, 15, 29. **Ralph Gates:** pages 18 (restaurant), 19, 28 (woman carrying cabbage). **M. Eugene Gilliom:** front cover (Kremlin), pages 1, 8, 9 (child with hat), 10 (Lenin's Tomb), 12, 13, 16, 17, 22, 23, 24, 25, 29 (shoppers in line).

Published by Willowisp Press, Inc.
401 E. Wilson Bridge Road, Worthington, Ohio 43085

Copyright©1990 by Willowisp Press, Inc.

All rights reserved. No portion of this book may be reproduced, stored in a retrieval system, or transmitted, in any form or by any means, electronic, mechanical, photocopying, recording or otherwise without prior written permission from the publisher.

Printed in the United States of America

10 9 8 7 6 5 4 3 2 1

ISBN 0-87406-453-8

This book is dedicated to the spirit of global friendship.

These Soviet and American youngsters have spent a week getting to know each other while attending summer camp in the Soviet Union. Here, on Arbat Street in Moscow, they play a game of friendship and cooperation, demonstrating that global friendship can be a reality.

Not many years ago, the Soviet Union was a mysterious place where the Communist "iron curtain" made it difficult for tourists from other countries to visit. Today, however, there is "glasnost," a Russian term meaning an openness to other countries, and the Soviet Union welcomes visitors from many foreign countries. In this photograph, a children's dance group is welcoming a group of visitors from the United States to Tbilisi in the republic of Georgia.

Because of glasnost, we have been able to learn much more about the people in the Soviet Union and their way of life. Let's take a look at what glasnost has shown us. Let's take a look around the Soviet Union.

If you were planning a trip to the Soviet Union, you would discover that it is the largest country in the world. The Soviet Union is so big that you would have to spend a week on a train to cross the country. You could cross the United States or Canada in approximately three days.

The Soviet Union is larger than Canada, the United Kingdom, and the United States combined. Like Canada, the Soviet Union is a northern country. In fact, Moscow is as far north as Sitka, Alaska.

The Union of the Soviet Socialist Republics (usually called the Soviet Union or the U.S.S.R.) is made up of 15 Soviet Socialist Republics (usually called S.S.R.s). As you can see, Russia is the largest republic. Moscow is the capital of Russia and the capital of the U.S.S.R.

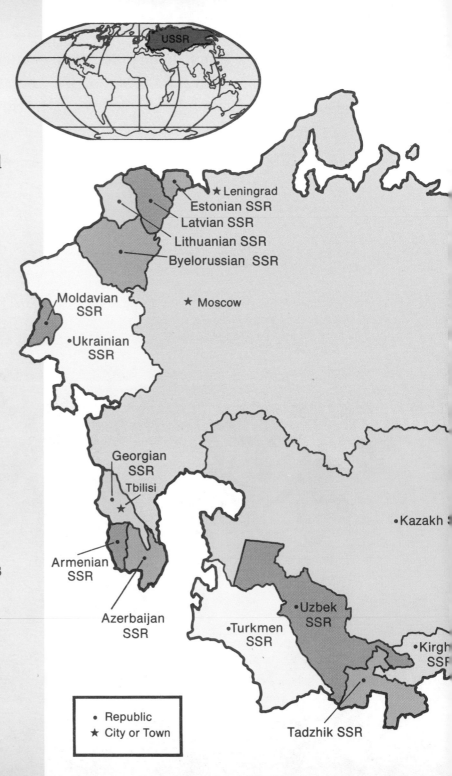

★ Leningrad
Estonian SSR
Latvian SSR
Lithuanian SSR
Byelorussian SSR

★ Moscow

Moldavian SSR

•Ukrainian SSR

Georgian SSR
Tbilisi

Armenian SSR

Azerbaijan SSR

•Kazakh

•Uzbek SSR

•Turkmen SSR

•Kirgh SSR

Tadzhik SSR

• Republic
★ City or Town

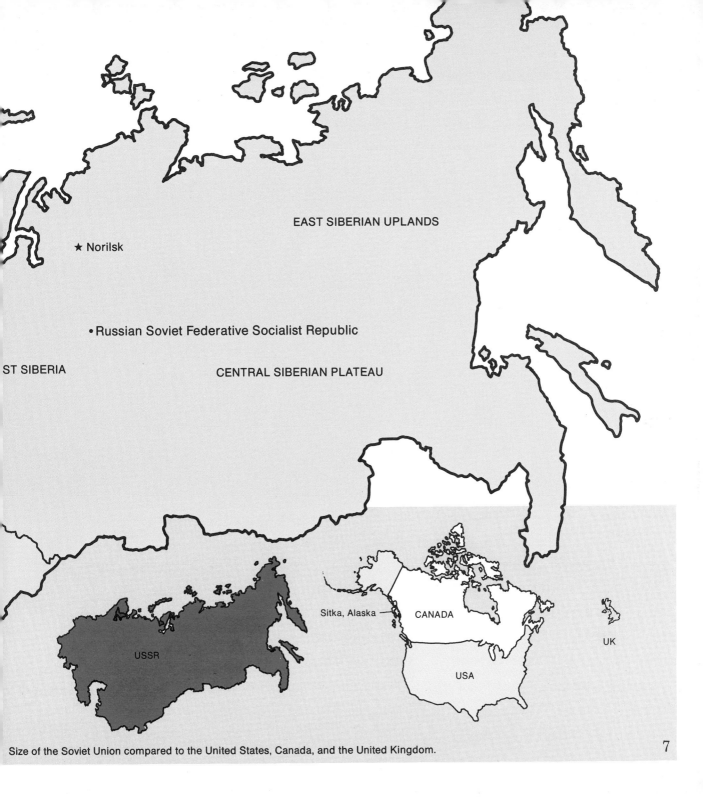

EAST SIBERIAN UPLANDS

★ Norilsk

•Russian Soviet Federative Socialist Republic

ST SIBERIA

CENTRAL SIBERIAN PLATEAU

Sitka, Alaska

CANADA

USSR

UK

USA

Size of the Soviet Union compared to the United States, Canada, and the United Kingdom.

About 280 million people live in the Soviet Union. This is the third largest population in the world. Only China and India have more people.

The people of the Soviet Union belong to more than 100 different nationalities. Each nationality has its own language, its own culture, and its own traditions. You can see in these pictures some of the differences in appearance and dress that are typical of the various nationalities.

Moscow is the largest city in the Soviet Union. Most people who visit Moscow want to see the Kremlin, the home of the Soviet government. Over 800 years ago, settlers began building a "Kreml," or walled fortress, around the most important buildings in their community. This "Kreml" grew into today's Kremlin, an area that contains government offices, museums, and churches (above photo).

The newest building in the Kremlin is the Kremlin Palace of Congresses (photo on left) where the Communist party and the Supreme Soviet meet. Under the eastern wall of the Kremlin is the tomb of Vladimir Lenin (photo on far left), the father of the Communist state. Red Square, where government parades are held, is next to the Kremlin.

Perhaps the most famous sight in Moscow is the four hundred-year-old St. Basil's Cathedral. The cathedral contains nine separate chapels, each with its own beautifully-decorated roof. Today the cathedral is a museum rather than a place of worship.

People from all over the Soviet Union visit Moscow. They cannot move there, though, unless they get permission from the government.

Because there is a housing shortage in Moscow, newly married couples usually have to live with their parents. A couple without children will often share their living space with another couple.

If you were to visit a typical family of four in Moscow, you would probably find them living in a two-room apartment in a large building. The family might have a black-and-white television set, but they would not have a telephone or a car.

Leningrad is the second largest city in the Soviet Union. The city, which was once named St. Petersburg, was the capital of Russia for over two hundred years. After the Communist Revolution of 1917, the city's name was changed to recognize Lenin, the leader of the revolution.

The city has many former palaces that belonged to early Russian rulers.

There are many beautiful and historic sites in Leningrad. Upper left, *Leningrad Hermitage*; lower left, *Leningrad Palace Square*; bottom, *Petrodvorets*; right, *Catherine's Palace*

The 55 million people who live in the union republics of Soviet Central Asia live very differently than the people in Moscow or Leningrad. These people are mostly Muslims who speak Turkish languages. Many of the people are shepherds.

The houses in Soviet Central Asia have raised platforms in one room where whole families sleep. In this restaurant people eat together on the raised platform.

18

19

Much of the Soviet Union is extremely cold. The Khanty people of Western Siberia (a part of the republic of Russia) make their clothes out of bear and reindeer skins. During much of the year, they use dogsleds as their primary means of travel.

In the town of Norilsk, the electric lights are turned on 24 hours a day during the winter because there is so little daylight.

Soviet children attend school for 10 years (from age six to sixteen) and most of them go to school six days a week. Every nationality has the right to attend school in its mother tongue, but all students must also study the Russian language.

Students wear uniforms in school. The badges on many of their uniforms are pictures of Lenin as a child. The back wall of the classroom also has a picture of Lenin. From the time they begin school, children are taught to recognize the founder of their nation.

Most youngsters between the ages of nine and fourteen belong to the Young Pioneers. Members of this group take a solemn oath to be loyal to the motherland, the Communist party, and communism. They wear the red scarf, a symbol of the Young Pioneers. In the summer members attend Young Pioneer camps. They also perform patriotic duties such as guarding the tomb of the unknown soldier.

Sports play an important role in Soviet life. In recent years, the Soviets have won more Olympic medals than any other country.

For over a hundred years, Russia has been a leader in ballet. Moscow's Bolshoi Ballet performs all over the world. Some of the most famous dancers in ballet companies throughout the world are Russian.

Talented children in the Soviet Union are chosen to go to special schools where they receive daily training in dance or in their sport.

If you were to shop in the Soviet Union, you might not be able to find such ordinary things as tooth-paste, fruit, or tennis shoes. You might even find many of the shelves empty! You would find food to eat and clothes to wear, but you wouldn't have many choices.

In a Communist country such as the Soviet Union, the government owns the land, shops, businesses, and farms. The government decides what crops to grow and what goods to produce. The Soviet government has not been able to produce enough goods or food for the people.

In 1985, Mikhail Gorbachev, General Secretary of the Communist Party of the Soviet Union and President of the U.S.S.R. Supreme Soviet, came into power in the Soviet Union. He introduced more freedom to the people and allowed them to begin owning small businesses. He began to shift government spending away from the military and toward products that people want and need. He began talks with leaders of other countries which have brought new hope for world peace. He started the new policy of friendship that allows young people of his country to become friends with youngsters from other lands.

GLOSSARY

communism. This term refers to a political system in which the government owns all the land, all the stores, all the businesses, and all the farms.

Communist party. The party that governs the Soviet Union and follows the Communist beliefs.

glasnost. This term means "openness." Because of glasnost, tourists may now enter the Soviet Union.

Gorbachev, Mikhail. The current leader of the Communist government.

Kremlin. This is the building that houses the Soviet government.

Lenin, Vladimir. This man led the Communist Revolution of 1917 and was very influential in helping develop the current government of the Soviet Union. He is often referred to as the father of the Communist state and was premier of the Soviet Union from 1917-1924.

Moscow. This is the largest city in the Soviet Union and is the capital of the Soviet Union.

Red Square. These are the grounds outside of the Kremlin where government parades are held.

republic. Any of the territorial and political units of the Soviet Union. The United States is divided into states, England is divided into counties, and the Soviet Union is divided into republics.

Supreme Soviet. A ruling body in the Soviet government made up of two equal houses. The Soviet of the Union is made up of members who are elected on the basis of population. The Soviet of Nationalities is made up of members elected by various nationality groups.

Young Pioneers. Youngsters between the ages of nine and fourteen belong to this organization and take a solemn oath to the motherland, the party, and communism. They attend a camp in the summer and perform patriotic duties.

INDEX

If you are interested in visiting the Soviet Union or in having a youngster from the Soviet Union visit you, write to:

- Kids Meeting Kids
  Box 8 H
  New York, NY 10025

- Youth Ambassadors
  of America
  P.O. Box 5273
  Bellingham, WA 98227

If you would like a pen pal, write to:

- Letters for Peace
  238 Autumn Ridge Rd.
  Fairfield, CT 06432

- Kids Talk to Kids
  MEND-P.O. Box 2309
  La Jolla, CA 92038

- Committee of Youth Organizations of the U.S.S.R
  61.Boqdana Khmelnitskovo 7/8
  Moscow, U.S.S.R.